The Dark Side of the Butterfly

A Collection of Poems

CJ Carter

THE DARK SIDE OF THE BUTTERFLY.

Copyright © 2024 All rights reserved— CJ Carter

No part of this book may be reproduced or transmitted in any form or by any means, graphic, electronic, or mechanical, including photocopying, recording, taping, or by an information storage retrieval system without the written permission of the publisher. The contents and cover of this book may not be reproduced in whole or in part in any form without the express written permission of the author or B.O.Y. Enterprises, Inc.

Please direct all copyright inquiries to:

B.O.Y. Publications, Inc.
c/o Author Copyrights
P.O. Box 262
Lowell, NC 28098
betonyourselfent.com

Paperback ISBN: 978-1-955605-72-4

Cover Design and Interior Illustrations: CYFR Studio, LLC

Interior Design: B.O.Y. Enterprises, Inc.

Printed in the United States.

Dedication

To Mommy and Daddy… thank you for always telling me I was loved and encouraging me to use my words and chase my dreams. Because of you… I am never afraid to speak out.

Life inspires. Poetry allows me to express the things my mind should not think… and my heart should not feel… to everyone or no one. Some poems are inspired by people I love and hold dear. Some are inspired by people I never liked. Some are based on events I never personally experienced but felt inspired to curate. Every poem paints a picture of a story that needed telling. These love notes, confessions and fantasies detail my metamorphosis as a storyteller, a poet, and a woman. Enjoy!

Table of Contents

Circle of Life 9
Day Dreaming 10
Charleston 11
Shortnin' Bread 12
T-E-R-S 13
Hidden Gems 14
Forgotten Tongue 15
As Trees Kissed the Ground 16
A Mother's Promise 17
Woman 19
Strong Men 20
Reminiscing 23
Sometimes Forgotten: Ode to Poetry 24
Captured Moment 26
Eyes Like Amber 27
Falling 28
Thank God for Speed Bumps 30
Her Hands 31
Honey 33
Lights Off 34
To Thine Own Self 35
Garden of Eden 37
Two Cups 38

Pink Walls 39

Haikus: Thoughts Not So Random 40

Thank You 42

Windows... 43

Love 44

Things Once Meant to be Remembered 45

Betrayal 46

Breaking... 47

Broken-Hearted Definitions 48

Just a Friend.. 49

Ex-Factor 50

How Do You? 52

Lingering Thoughts 54

Spitting Fire 56

But You Love Him 58

Spiritual Healing 60

Choices 62

Clock on the Wall 63

Equilibrium 64

Every Five Minutes... 66

Fear 67

Forgotten Queens.. 68

From the View Up Top 70

Life in a 6X9 72

Like Magic... 73

Reality Check 74

Seeing Red	75
Solid Rock	77
Comparison	79
Unspoken Truths	80
Coming Out	82
Afterthoughts	84
Blackness	85
Good Hair (reprised)	87
Black History	89
Family Tree	90
A Shout-Out	91
As Seen Through Black Eyes	93
Election Day: 11/04/08	94
Barack and Michelle: At Last	95
Necklace	97
Proud to be American	98
Stand Your Ground	100
Soaring High	102
Poet's Warning	105
About the Author	106
If These Pages	108

Butterflies are beautiful, graceful creatures that go through four stages of development. It can take a butterfly anywhere from one month to one year to complete all four stages.

In the end… everyone celebrates the beauty of the butterfly, but most people never acknowledge what it went through to get there.

PART 1: EGG

The Beginning

Circle of Life

We live in darkness before light
trapped and cradled,
kicking all the time
wanting out desperately
anticipating that big push
that will give us a chance
to live for the first time
in a light we learn will end
in sudden darkness.

Day Dreaming

I am creative and poetic.
I wonder why people waste opportunities.
I hear summer whispers during winter nights.
I see the colors of the wind.
I want to be an example worth following.
I am a lyrical artist.

I pretend to care when I sometimes don't.
I feel like laughing at funerals.
I touch the irony of life with numb fingers.
I worry that I won't be good enough.
I cry when my stifled tears overflow.
I am creative and poetic.

I understand that a life without love is pointless.
I know everything happens for a reason.
I dream about one day proving "Them" wrong.
I live my words and speak truth.
I hope I make a difference in this world.
I am beautiful and authentic.

Charleston

Cherished oak trees
dressed in Spanish moss,
renowned gardens and plantations,
the city of hospitality…
that's Charleston.

Red rice and candied yams,
okra soup, oysters and clams,
the soul in soul food…
that's Charleston.

Leisure walks along the Waterfront.
Sunday, ice cream at the battery.
The place where muggy summers
fall before warm winters…
that's Charleston.

Shortnin' Bread

I remember his voice roaring from the kitchen.
"Y'all kids want some shortnin' bread?"
The sound of six small feet stampeding
broke the silence that filled the house.
Shortnin' Bread was Daddy's treat—
thick slices drenched in syrup
sticking to the roofs of our mouths.
Gooey fingers and glowing faces
never made me suspect then
that Shortnin' Bread was a poor man's creation
disguised as a late-night snack
to spare his children the disappointment
of going to bed hungry.

T-E-R-S

Designed and detailed
three consonants and a vowel
embedded in a half moon.
Daisy decorated.
Lifeless letters
evoking a range of emotions,
colorful memories,
and kept secrets.
Authentic Italian purposely separated
symbolizing a bond
not meant to be broken…
S-I-S.

Hidden Gems

Family is what you make of it.
Relationships that bring you joy.
Bonds that bind when love exists.

Favoring characteristics.
Playful girls and rambunctious boys.
Family is what you make of it.

Anticipated visits.
Aunts and uncles bearing toys.
Bonds that bind when love exists.

More than blood defines relatives.
Treasured friendships proven loyal.
Family is what you make of it.

Laughable moments and ego trips.
Those whose caring is not a ploy.
Bonds that bind when love exists.

Outshining pain that inward lives.
Valued gems hidden in soil.
Family is what you make of it.
Bonds that bind when love exists.

Forgotten Tongue

I've spent the majority of my life
on a small rural island
making decisions I thought were right,

hoping to escape the darkness of night
since ignorance forces the mouth silent.
I've spent the majority of my life

hiding from stereotypes
placed on the residents of the island.
Making decisions I thought were right.

My accent would not hinder me if light.
Heavy Geechee sounds slurred and rugged.
I've spent the majority of my life

contemplating how I'd have to fight
since my native tongue did not blend.
Making decisions I thought were right.

I sometimes regret speaking "proper and right"
as if I were never from The Island, where
I've spent the majority of my life
making decisions I thought were right.

As Trees Kissed the Ground

It snowed.
It snowed.
Flakes of white
in January
generating cancellations
slowing traffic
warming hearts
answering child-like prayers
building snowmen
while playing hooky
and drinking hot chocolate
after aiming tightly packed
balls of white
at friends and strangers
who ducked alike
smiling, laughing, and retaliating,
treasuring that moment
when differences and difficulties
did not matter.
At that very moment
as trees kissed the ground
and…
It snowed.
It snowed.

A Mother's Promise

My story…
is woven throughout history
but often goes untold.
Simple sacrifices synonymous with
a mother's love, a wife's devotion, a sister's loyalty…
attributions and affirmations, I regularly embody.

My middle name is Strength,
but I am sometimes mistaken for Weakness.

Physical limitations exploit my talents
and surrender tears when my pain is too much.
With His help, I conceived the miracle of Hope
and carried her 9 months,
270 days and 6,480 hours
until she tore her way into this world
kicking and screaming, splitting and tearing,
yet still I managed to praise God
for every agonizing moment.

Her middle name is Tomorrow.

My job is to nurture and protect

The Dark Side of the Butterfly- The Beginning

guide, love and embrace everything she is
and anything she is not.
I will not fail.

Our future depends on her surviving
years of abuse and neglect
embedded within a society that chooses
to misrepresent her defenses as flaws,
leaving her with wounded pride
second guessing her worth.
She is both precious and priceless.
Like a diamond under pressure,
she will slice through defeat
redefining the image of beauty
emerging from a pit of lies empowered,
a survivor walking in her own truth.

And her story…
her story will be shouted from mountain tops
and whispered through valleys,
repeated for centuries to come
in tongues of every language
revealing to the world
a beautiful creation of God.

Woman

Woman…
strong, nurturing
beautiful and dynamic.
Able to endure
complicated pregnancies,
painful deliveries,
misinformed and misguided
men.
Closing gender gaps,
crossing boundaries
all while remaining
seductive and alluring.
Possessing answers to questions
men are afraid to ask.
Perhaps God created her second
to save His best for last.

Strong Men

We love them.
Strong men
born of the earth,
unique in form
possessing hearts larger than life.
Correctors of wrong,
willing to sacrifice.

We need them.

Strong men
built to last.
Tough like rock
they won't break like glass.
When times get hard
and despair fills the air
they will never show an inkling of fear.
Priceless is their love
worn on their sleeves
protective like a glove
deeper than the ocean is deep.

We cherish them.

Strong men
beautiful and rare,
incredible husbands,
outstanding fathers,
persevering leaders,
remarkable teachers.
The epitome of strength
that comes from within,
showing their daughters
how to be queens
and their sons
how to be kings.

We miss them.

Strong men
gracing us with a presence
than can only be God sent.
When these warriors go home to rest
we shed many tears but never forget
their legacy or lives
vividly retold.
Honored through memories
more valuable than gold.
Heroes who set the standard
for others to follow,

planting seeds of pride
that will bear fruit tomorrow.

Strong men.
We thank God for them.

Reminiscing

Hope grows old
when it seems dark days
outnumber the good
and memories begin to fade
like pictures of Grandma
when she was young and pretty;
a lot slimmer in those days
before she had a husband
and nine little mouths to feed.
Every Sunday was Thanksgiving
covering the table
with dressing and greens,
filling the rooms of the small house
stable in the warmth it provided,
a sanctuary to all who entered
living, loving, laughing
'till the end.

Sometimes Forgotten: Ode to Poetry

I thought we were one,
synonymous with the other.
Finding your presence in everything I do,
I loved you completely.
Allowing me, a small stream
to flow into waters
unsurmountable by others,
I followed you blindly
guided only by faith and emotions.
You held me steadfast when I felt us drifting,
becoming distant friends…
mere strangers among a page of words.
And when the darkness
nearly consumed me,
you lit the path
that saved my life.

PART 2: MOLTING

The Shedding

Captured Moment

Lying head on breast

fingers lightly stroking hair.

Innocent play on a public bench.

A tickle produces laughter

seductively concealed with a kiss.

Two bodies.

Two hearts.

Synchronized

to love.

Eyes Like Amber

Eyes like amber beam intensely
seducing my soul,
making love to my mind,
leaving passionate thoughts
and appetites to be fed.
Quenching your thirst
with my organic juices,
I yearn for your touch
with hands soft as satin,
embracing my bare curves
filling me with your love
until my cup overflows.

Falling

I fell…
Slowly at first not realizing I was falling
until I was mid-fall and forced to decide
should I brace myself or take the full impact,
accepting responsibility for the consequences
that would follow if I allowed gravity and nature
to take its course.

I fell…
closing my eyes and praying
I would be able to block out the pain
I may soon experience,
acknowledging that a broken wrist
would not hurt as much as a bruised heart.
Choosing to end my falling would be easy
if finding out what happens once I stand again
did not arouse my curiosity.

I fell…
trusting you would catch me…
shaken, hurting, confused,
seeing me for the first time…
someone beautiful worth pursuing.

And in those brief seconds,
I fell…in love.

Thank God for Speed Bumps

Ever driven over a speed bump without braking?
Felt your tires leave the pavement,
soaring briefly through the air
creating that tingling sensation
that rushes over your body
slightly edging your grasp on control
right before landing on pavement,
acknowledging that you never slowed down
purposely enjoying every second
of unrestrained exhilaration?
No?
Ever made love to woman?

Her Hands

A slow melody pours
from the speakers of the clock radio
as hands travel down the small of my back
communicating a relaxed sense of peace,
relieving tension onset by the monotony
of a day's work.
These healing hands
massage away years of pain
evident in pre-mature wrinkles,
tell-tale signs of a hard-lived life,
and are nothing in comparison to
the abusive ones that stole innocence
producing the false belief
that sex equaled love,
a lesson few parents take time to teach.
These faithful hands
have become my drug of choice,
calming my troubles and restless mind
of the doubt and shame
placed on relationships labeled indecent.
Hopeless are those who conform to titles
rather than submitting to the truth of their hearts.
Once removed, I long for the strength

The Dark Side of the Butterfly- The Shedding

and happiness captured by
those nurturing hands
similar to mine
seeking serenity and understanding.

Honey

Honey…
is the color of your eyes
when the sun catches them
dancing to the tune of my voice
at the sound of the words…
I love you.
Honey…
though thick and sticky,
is a tasteful delight when warmed and poured
delicately over your body
from the peak of your breasts
filling your navel then down to the delta
where the river has started flowing.
Honey…
is more than a term of endearment
when referring to you.
It is the beauty of your smile
accented by the curve of your hips
and the softness of your skin
when you lay in my arms.
It is the song two lovers make
when the sound of ecstasy
is the only music.

Lights Off

Incense and candles burning sweet hypnotic fragrances.
Pink and red petals sprinkled throughout the room.
Two lovers dancing.
Seductive melodies setting the mood.
Supple lips kissing bare flesh
finding… secret hot places.
Two become one as sheets rise and fall.
One pause to find those eyes
which say more than words can
and the rise and fall
beneath the sheets
begin
again.

To Thine Own Self

Beautiful brown eyes
stare back intimidating me
while expecting answers to the questions
no one dared to ask.
These eyes know
the secrets I have kept
and the lies I have told
to the lovers I have shared.
They see beyond the hardened exterior
and gaze into the spiritual
realm of my being,
seeking peace within,
but often finding
massive shades of gray
encompassing thoughts and emotions
both black and white,
having a penguinistic effect
before merging into one
combined concoction of confusion
being poured in martini glasses
and served as a happy hour cocktail.

These hypnotic eyes seek the truth

The Dark Side of the Butterfly- The Shedding

education alone cannot provide.
They analyze the colors of the rainbow
which, individually, do not mean much
until brought together on decals
celebrating unions between lovers
willing to defy society's definition
of acceptable relationships.
These warm eyes engage the heart
in an intense game of hide and seek
while freedom is sought
in a trial where love
stands accused.

Garden of Eden

I am the delicate center
of a forbidden fruit.
Sweet on the inside,
my nectar drizzles over
the curves of your cheek
when you devour me whole.
Intoxicating is my fragrance
luring you closer
until the temptation to taste
surpasses the need to touch
my smooth, textured surface.
After a gentle fondling
to determine ripeness,
you consume me,
savoring the flavor
of my sensual fruit.

Two Cups

Soft lips convey
secrets of the heart
purposely concealed,
embedded in codes
beguiling to most
as sensual glances
across the room
release beautiful butterflies
in an array of colors
gracefully fluttering throughout my body
teasing nerves and creating pools
of erotic fantasies of drowning you.
You are the sugar to my coffee-
a deep rich blend and enticing aroma.
Two cups a day
leave me breathless,
stroking the edge of anticipation,
foreplay at the corners of your mouth.
While subtle smiles provoke orgasmic promises
and once again, I am lost in you.

Pink Walls

I find pink walls alluring.
Delicate and gentle,
they create unique depth
surrounding me with warmth
inviting my touch,
manifesting an atmosphere so intoxicating
it teases while piquing curiosity
trespassing on dangerous territory
allowing imaginary boundaries to be crossed
in heated moments of weakness.
Pink walls pulsate when swollen
releasing a nectar potent and seductive
momentarily dismissing beliefs, vows, and promises
climaxing to reach a place
where broken hearts
no longer matter.

Haikus: Thoughts Not So Random

Never accept no
when a yes is required
to appease your soul.

                      Ticking clocks breath truth
                      as frantic moments linger
                      and my dreams depart.

Correction sometimes
bruise feelings and warrant change,
but growth is needed.

                      Aging is like wine;
                      wet and dry, bitter and sweet-
                      an acquired taste.

PART 3: CHRYSALIS

The Metamorphasis

Thank You

Thank you for breaking my heart
in a million pieces.
Through the pieces,
I experienced pain…
sharp, fierce, and relentless.
But through the pain,
I found myself…
sharp, fierce, and relentless.

Windows

Sand burnt at hundreds of degrees
creates art often unappreciated.
Installed in our homes,
offices and valued possessions,
they provide more than a look at nature's canvas
where brilliant whites waltz across baby blues
accented by orange, yellow and red hues
indicating a changing of the seasons.
They manifest boundaries
between things constant and those uncontrolled,
producing the illusion of flowers blooming
at your bedside within an arm's reach
without the frustration of muggy mornings
or nippy nights.
Eye candy for the visually glycemic,
affirming an ageless rule…
look, but don't touch.
Touching leaves traces of your existence
smudged or streaked across what once held
the appearance of crystal-clear perfection
now sullied with prints of tempted palms
desiring more than just a view.

Love

Ever tried using a butter knife
to cut a steak?
A difficult task.
The steak is tough,
but even when tender,
the butter knife is too blunt,
too smooth on both sides.
With effort, it could eventually
break through the soul of the meat.
But why bother with the headache?
Butter knives are not meant to cut steaks.

Things Once Meant to be Remembered

The shredding machine
shreds notes,
secret memos,
personal messages;
things once meant
to be remembered
all gone, torn
into long white strips,
blue strips, pink
and yellow too.
The color does not matter.
For after it reaches
the teeth of the machine
it is never to be seen
whole again.

Betrayal

Piercing through flesh
the smooth blade gently glides
severing nerves,
ripping through organs,
destroying muscles,
stealing life.
The chest tightens.
Breathing quickens.
and misery smiles
in response to the betrayal.
Crying is the only solace
to a trampled heart,
forever scarred
by thoughtless footprints.

Breaking

There's nothing
like the sound of glass
hitting a wall
shattering
scattering
sharpened
pieces
jagged
and imprecise.
Different points of entry
ripping
slicing
tearing
flesh and emotions
numbing the pain
unrelieved by apologies
that fade like photos
once feelings are appeased,
a Machiavellian solution
justifying the means
since no one likes the sound of sirens
accompanied by blue lights
that waken nosy neighbors
in the middle of the night.

Broken-Hearted Definitions

Love-
Often used as an excuse
after hurting someone devoted
and committed to another.
In love-
A condition that affects hormones,
altering moods, influencing decisions…
only curable with time,
leaving internal scars
that never fully heal.
Single-
Unadulterated freedom;
being rid of dead weight
and unnecessary heart ache;
a choice to actively seek companionship
from another more worthy than the last.

Just a Friend

Secluded in a dark room,
lonely thoughts catalyst
mixed emotions creating confusion
as sexual frustration
and broken promises resurface
along with hidden fears.
Trust can be lost
more easily than gained
when signatures are left
engraved on your neck.
Forgiving does not equate forgetting.
Only time can appease pain
while thoughtless actions continue
producing wet pillow cases
and swollen red eyes
much like the red illuminating this room
indicating yet again,
Extension In Use.

Ex-Factor

I hate that I'm still in love with you
after all the lies,
remembering the times
I nearly drowned crying over why
you weren't here or there or where
you said you'd be.
Waiting patiently, I anticipated the day
you'd realize the lustful illusion of love
you sought in the horizon
had already dawned
and was lying beside you
curved to your body,
providing a warmth more comforting
than any expensive duvet.
So many nights you'd roll over
kissing my lips softly,
stroking and caressing
peaks and crevices,
waking me to fill my body,
leaving us both breathless and sweating,
clinging to each other.
I still crave those intimate sessions
along with the way your eyes lit up

The Dark Side of the Butterfly- The Metamorphosis

when I entered a room,
proudly announcing to the world
that I belonged to you,
but more importantly,
you belonged to me.

How Do You?

How do you let go
when you have loved so long and so hard
that all you know is how to be together?
How do you hold back tears
that flow so effortlessly
at the thought of being apart
despite the obvious pain
that manifest them?
How do you keep your head up and move on
when the one who taught you to love
is the same who taught
the meaning of heartache and pain?
How do you look forward to brighter days
when your heart and mind
can't remember the last time
you were happy?
How do you find peace within
and hold onto faith that one day
your smile will return
forgetting the stranger you had become
after recognizing the beauty of your spirit
no longer stifled by lies and deceit
Evident in the joy that pours from your eyes

The Dark Side of the Butterfly- The Metamorphosis

even when they are closed.
How do you learn to trust again
after your feelings have been dismissed
as if your sacrifices and devotion meant nothing?
How do you get out of your own way
so you can live life presently
appreciating the disappointments
as much as the blessings
that often come concealed
in moments of despair?
How do you?

Lingering Thoughts

My heart's capacity to love manifests innocuous
thoughts tugging at curiosities within speed limits
racing past warnings on this endless highway of residual
disappointment peaking its ugly head wearing purple
colored Jellies from youth that must
be replaced with stilettos and desires that ring

of womanhood living in a broken ring
of trust. Me loving you loving me should be innocuous
save for suspicions that whisper. Doubt must
be the result of soft-spoken lies tempting hard limits
meant to ease a guilty conscience and prevent purple
bruises that bleed through residual

traces of Covergirl, the residual
concealer of battered egos and abandoned rings
of commitment appeased by purple
roses left on a bedside table, an innocuous
gesture or admission of guilt after testing the limits
of my forgiveness which festers and nettles like must

trapped in a sauna. Happiness must
allude faint-hearted fools relying on residual
love to fill voids created when fidelity limits

The Dark Side of the Butterfly- The Metamorphosis

are encroached upon and regret rings,
imposing on once innocuous
friendships founded on favorites live the color purple.

I deserve a purple
heart for surviving you and must
have mistaken the gales of our love for an innocuous
storm passing through leaving residual
signs of broken relationships encircled in rings
of fallen friendships scattered throughout city limits.

Silently destroying trust while manifesting limits
I dared my soul to cross, you hustled purple
haze and false promises beneath a platinum ring
convincing my heart to ignore the must
fragranced, lies assaulting my senses and residual
hope that I could be all you needed, an innocuous

plea offered and rejected in the ring of love and limits
creating innocuous attempts at hating those purple
roses, a residual reminder that you must have loved me.

Spitting Fire

Arrogance was not the game you played
when trying to win my heart
with your therapeutic ballads
promising a blissful eternity in paradise.
There was no mention
of baby mamas or jealous exes, in general,
sadistic women spreading unnecessary drama,
threatening to bulldoze the union
we rigorously tried to build.
I expressed what I thought was love,
ignoring countless zodiac warnings
of our incompatibility.
You were the tempest that disrupted my world,
flooding my soul with emotions unimaginable
only to arrive at a disappointing climax
once the recidivism of your deceit became apparent,
transforming this tranquil butterfly
into a raging phoenix,
epitomizing a woman scorned.
Unsatisfied with your worthless apologies of wasted
breath,
I pause briefly remembering…
 a tender moment almost forgotten

before promptly returning to hating you.
A pleasant smile flashes across these vengeful eyes
concealing my aggression and tainted thoughts of truth
as I sinfully contemplate....
you're not bullet proof.

But You Love Him

Words can't describe the passion in his eyes
that pours out in silent tears when he holds you.
You love the strength of his hands, weathered and worn
from doing a man's work…whatever that is,
irrelevant to most as long as the bills get paid.
Yes, money rules the world
causing disillusioned children
to believe happiness can be bought
or hidden behind bruised knuckles
left after creating bloody noses
when dinner was burnt or late or simply
not what he wanted.
Guilt and innocence become so interchangeable
that you accept blame and mask scars
with phony smiles and extra makeup
while closing ears to encouragement to walk away.
Maybe your desperation for love
manifested this dependency on his sex and violence
which have manipulated your mind
sprouting weeds of deception
that need to be plucked before they outgrow
the seeds of self-worth planted many years ago.
No amount of ecstasy can ever justify

The Dark Side of the Butterfly- The Metamorphosis

the fear in your eyes
that pours out in painful tears
when he holds you
tightly
by the neck,
stifling
your
last
breath
with those strong,
masculine hands
you mistook for love.

Spiritual Healing

Spiritual healing is what you call
the way his hands caress
those places tense and tight,
frustrated from a day's work
and a woman's needs.
Brilliant memories of what used to be
the ambitious lover who made you weak
are replaced with sensuous images
cloaked in infidelity.
Spiritual healing is how you justify
succumbing to another man's kiss
labeled as innocent
until you leave his bed
satisfied and seeking
less and more.

PART 4 : IMAGO

The Rebirth

Choices

Seduction plus sperm equals suicide
of his irresponsibility while trying to be
the man I need him to be,
the man she already calls daddy,
a man worthy of the title
with no role models to follow.
Accustomed to the fuck-you-and-leave,
no pamper buying,
when-he-ain't-eating, he's cheating
man who fathered him.
A product of government cheese and housing
minus confidence and ambition
equals a lifetime of struggling
too painful to pass on.
Contemplating the right move to make
as he paces and waits
for one dot or two, a pink strip or blue
builds anticipation, regret
and the possibility of doubling his burdens.
Seduction plus sperm equals bad choices
that often lead to suicide of a man's hopes and dreams,
producing the tears he's taught not to shed.

Clock on the Wall

Hands ticking away-
9:00
eyes searching the room.
The door is locked.

A million thoughts
running through my mind
past due notices stacked high
bare tables and dinner sighs
still don't help
pass the time.

Guilty of a moral crime.
Using resources mama gave,
seeking the bottom of my grave.
Diminishing options is the cause.

Maternal obligations
warrant the situation.
Broken ring of commitment.
Mistakes made-
9:15
rent is paid.

Equilibrium

Preadolescent circumstances
scarred her walls, distorting views
of green pastures
nonexistent
except for in dreams
where monsters could be frightened
and mothers protected their daughters.
Congenital disappointments
exposed her to a world
where innocence and hope
were buried alive,
exasperating her patience
while waiting on miracles that never came.
Flabbergasted by the indolence
of individuals sworn to protect,
she refused to cooperate with a system
successfully destroying the pockets of faith
she had managed to obtain
from the parents of her own,
the only example
of unadulterated love she knew.
Anti-social disorder-
 the terminology used

to describe her fascination
with lies and manipulation,
destructive tendencies to abuse
friendships and relationships,
revealing a scared little girl
who once dreamed of silver-plated coffins
that offered optimistic opportunities
to escape Hell with evacuation routes
since happy endings
only exist in fairy tales.

Every Five Minutes

Time is man's best friend.
Although lacking physical features,
it's more corruptive than money,
more destructive than any weapon.
With time man can know everything,
control everyone, and destroy anything
once considered sacred, precious, and priceless.
Time is a woman's greatest enemy.
With it she,
God's most magnificent creation,
can be destroyed.

Fear

Fear looks like a mother
clinging onto hope at the side
of her newborn's incubator.
Fear sounds like the silence
that rings after a monitor flat-lines
and a wife is left
without her soul mate.
Fear feels like the sting of reality
that pains leaders and teachers
burdened by despair at the thought of tomorrow
being led by the youth of today.
Fear tastes like the sweat that rolls
from a quivering brow
as anxiety builds,
knowing either success or failure
will be the outcome.

Forgotten Queens

Remember me?
I am the bag lady you saw on the street
living off of scraps.
The hag you witnessed collecting cans
begging day after day with soiled hands.
While you laughed and spat in my face,
I am the one society seemed to hate.

Remember me?
I am the whore you paid last night
to satisfy your sexual appetite.
The fiend who needed her fix
even if it meant sexing to get it.
Degrading my body for your nocturnal pleasures,
I am the one who fucked you better.

Remember me?
I am the bitch who bore your children.
Good enough to suck your dick but not wear your ring.
The one you beat when things didn't go right
and abandoned when money was tight.
Struggling to survive every day,
I was the one left to explain why daddy went away.

The Dark Side of the Butterfly- The Rebirth

Remember me?
I am the queen who was loved by all.
Confident of my strengths, I stood proud and tall.
The symbol of dignity for every woman,
a nurturer and protector of all children.
Portrayed as the essence of beauty and respect,
I am the one you all must never forget.

From the View Up Top

From the view up top
nature seems at piece
running its course
undisturbed by man's
burden of technology
or greed to achieve
the comfort of the Joneses,
a stereotype.
No one notices the small ripples
until a splash occurs
unsettling the surface,
a mirror of disappointment
hidden by smiles
painted and plastic,
a mask.
Water is supposed to cleanse
not overwhelm the body,
filling the lungs,
submerging the soul
too weakened by frustration
to struggle or fight,
submitting to the blurry
view up top

The Dark Side of the Butterfly- The Rebirth
where natures seems at peace,
running its course
undisturbed.

Life in a 6X9

Looking out the window seems so simplistic;
almost too ridiculous to waste a prayer on.
Mine are numbered so I use them sparingly
minus those times when restless thoughts whisper,
"God, please don't let them see me."
There is no difference between night and day
when you can't see the sun or feel its warmth.
No summer kisses or winter smiles.
Just mundane movement seducing my curiosity
as I catch a glimpse of others being productive.
Irony beats me daily, stripping away pieces of my sanity,
risking what little freedom is given
to be trapped in this rectangular cage
once desperation and despair fuse,
and I get caught looking out the window,
all the while secretly praying,
"God, please don't let them see me."

Like Magic

I reside in the eyes
of the one you love,
but you never see me.
Playing carelessly
like children in the street,
I thrive when you release your inhibitions,
momentarily forgetting
the definition of safe
when describing love
in a foolish attempt
to proclaim trust.
Like a chameleon,
I transform blending perfectly
to conceal the truth.
Ignorance is my strongest ally,
increasing and decreasing
numbers simultaneously.
I am a murderer
mirrored as a myth,
and I may already
be living inside you.

Reality Check

Reality is that stray bullet that imbeds itself
in the skull of a nine-year-old
running errands after ten
to help his crack addicted mother
support her habit.
Often painful,
reality is what keeps us from drifting away
to a world where dreams come true,
bills are paid on time
and the price of happiness is affordable.
Always true,
reality paints a picture even the blind can see,
putting life into perspective
by taking away the difficulty in prioritizing.
Usually unexpected,
reality leaves footprints
after treading over
the lovely illusions life allows us.
Reality is that intentional bullet
that sprays white walls red
when all else fails
and faith alone is not enough.

Seeing Red

Boredom usually overcrowds
the walls of my mind,
but today they sway with ease
alternating between thoughts
of reality and fantasy.
The what-ifs have taken over,
compelling me to sit when I should run.
Decisions to make…
eliminate the fun
or at least the sun
that used to shine,
in spite of the clouds surrounding me.
Announcement.
Rejection.
Disappointment.
Reflection.
That is the order that caught
this perfectly flawed butterfly
in a blood-stained net
when the sounds of chaos and hysteria
awoke the room like a siren
and I felt for the first time
a kick from within

The Dark Side of the Butterfly- The Rebirth

lift the lead in my feet and move me.
Flashes of white soiled with splashes of red
is all that I remember
as I leaped across tables and chairs,
friends and foes, obstacles that dared
to threaten our safety
since for now we are one
in an equation that ends with two
and you are the greater variable.

Solid Rock

Sometimes out of nowhere
I feel you push
deep from within my soul
reaching through the sea of no possibilities
touching me in places previously untouched.
Relinquished dreams come rushing back
diluted by salty streams
distorting my foundation
as I gasp trying to conceal
that pit of emptiness overwhelming
the space in my throat,
suffocating the hope of normalcy.

I am a rock,
and rocks don't cry
so instead I shift my weight
and fill my mind with thoughts
of any and every… thing but you,
reciting my fickle list of cons
secretly despising those moms
that don't deserve the chance
I will never get.

The Dark Side of the Butterfly- The Rebirth

I hate feeling inadequate
incapable of forgetting the names I chose.
Little girl fantasies
dismissed by real life occurrences
unscripted, unrehearsed, unfair.
Sometimes out of nowhere
I feel you reaching,
and I reach back choking yearnful tears
that get lighter over the years
but never disappear
even though
I am a rock,
and rocks don't cry.

Comparison

Rain and pain
both can fall unexpectedly
varying in amounts.
Meteorologists and psychics
try to predict the two
sometimes successfully.
Not that knowing in advance
makes it easier to accept
the droplets of water
that seep through the thin
mushroom shaped nylon
held to shield yourself
while your heart bleeds
uncovered and raw
after watching them lower
the body of one you loved.
Six feet might as well be a million.
Yes, pain and rain
both can fall
unexpectedly
varying in amounts.

Unspoken Truths

Sometimes I just want to live
in a bubble of unspoken truths
where hurt feelings and sad expressions don't exist
since you're never in your feelings
or feeling deflated after hearing
the answers to questions
your heart hid from you.

That place where you feel full and focused
on chasing those elusive dreams
you think still may come true
if you chase them longer,
wish for them harder,
write them down and pray for them more.
The place you get before you get
overwhelmed by reality and financial strain
accompanied by the dream stealers
you call enemies, family, and friends
who are tired of hearing about these…
never-gonna-happen-in your-lifetime dreams.

That bubble that convinces you
that you haven't yet failed

even though you have accomplished nothing
and create new goals daily
since yesterday's goals weren't met
and tomorrow's deadlines are quickly approaching.
That space between wrong and right...
where darkness, light, and consequences haven't collided...
where everything gets quiet and you proudly smile thinking...
Damn, that shit worked...
Before disappointment and despair come crashing in,
pinning you against a wall.

That bubble of unspoken truth
keeps your heart beating
when your soul wants to slip
into an emotionally-induced coma
to protect what is left of it
after life is done slitting your wrists,
leaving you weakened and bleeding out.
It tells you that you will recover,
reminds you that you are a survivor,
picks you up off the blood-stained floors,
cleans your wounds,
and repeats a mantra of affirmations
necessary to inflate your ego,
giving you the desire
to keep pushing on.

Coming Out

Stumbling after last night's drinks,
memories crawl from buried places revealing secrets
too bothersome to keep. Symbols of love
viewed through double-sided glasses
Send reflections of denial
surfacing above anxious tears.

I shudder remembering my Father's tears
staining my heart's linen like red wine. Drinks
guzzled in anticipation of his denial.
Shaken nerves expelled secret
declarations poured in tall glasses
looking half-empty, replenished by love.

How will I survive without their love?
Boasting ultimatums, impending tears.
My near-sighted fears need glasses
of cranberry-chased drinks
to weed through lies and oppressive secrets.
I silently shouted at their denial.

Ubiquitous admissions of truth overshadowed by denial
willing to sacrifice it all for love.

The Dark Side of the Butterfly- The Rebirth

Falling on a sword of seductive secrets,
empowered to embrace emotions that tear
thoughts away from celebratory drinks,
and toasts of champagne in monogrammed glasses.

I decided to take off my glasses
choosing blurred vision over denial,
refusing to allow my soul to drink
poisoned cocktails of unaccepted love.
Victimized while society tears apart
the essence of my happiness, birthing secrets.

I aborted those secrets
pouring my sins in communion glasses
seeking acceptance through pained tears
released after years of denial
no longer afraid to profess my love
inebriated with her passion-filled drinks

replacing those tears with smiles after secrets
ebb and my heart drinks acceptance from glasses
once filled with denial, now emptied by love.

Afterthoughts

Picturing your eyes
brown like mine,
bright and wide
eager to see the world
all in once glance.
Hesitant to blink
out of fear of missing
something or someone,
brings a smile to my face
soon followed by tears.
Realizing we will never meet,
flesh of my flesh
seed from my womb.
Denied opportunity
by what was considered
"the more favorable" of its kind,
forced the decision,
less of a choice,
to sacrifice the possibility
of creating your life
to selfishly continue mine.

Blackness

Blackness is a state of mind.
It is earned, and is not present at birth.
It is only acquired by those willing
to risk obtaining it.
Blackness is power,
a culmination of inner and outer strength;
The ability to express oneself eloquently
In the midst of debate with actions and words.
Blackness is not synonymous with darkness or evil.
Instead it is a combination of everything
that makes living complete,
a union of mind, heart and soul.

Why not call it Whiteness?

Whiteness by definition symbolizes innocence,
a lie told and exposed through history.
To achieve Blackness one must dip
in the temptation of correcting history,
removing generational shackles,
savoring the rich flavor of retribution
while resisting being devoured by its existence.
Blackness is a self-confidence

stronger than any force.
Once obtained
it cannot
be destroyed.
Blackness is.

Good Hair (reprised)

Nappy, kinky
bush on my head
snagging fingers,
breaking teeth-
"Quote Unquote"
I don't have good hair.

"Good Hair" lies flat
submits and is obedient,
however, my fro fights back
against heat and chemicals
protesting the injustice
of white creams on black coils
eventually losing the battle-
"Quote Unquote"
I don't have good hair.

Mine is the thickly matted
hair of my ancestors
without traces of their infidel massahs.
Strong locs of love,
a symbol of resistance.
Never silky straight,

only defiant natural curls.
I don't have their hair.

This peezy mane belongs to me,
It's mine to control.
Despite its coarse nature
and uncoiffed appearance
I'm perfectly content that
"Quote Unquote"
I don't have "Good Hair."

Black History

Basically
learning to
appreciate the
cultural advances of
key individuals
historically dismissed
immeasurably by
society's prejudice
through events of the past
outlined and recorded,
retelling
yesterday's trials today, inspiring tomorrow.

Family Tree

Many years passed
before I learned of your importance
and how your past shaped my existence.
Our roots are entwined in decades of disgrace.
My ancestor's pride you willingly defaced,
allowing their persecutors,
oppressive and mad,
ultimately to have the last laugh.

Oh, Oak you stand here still strong
unable to feel the guilt of your unconscious wrong.
Providing limbs from which children playfully swung
and my ancestors unlawfully hung.

A Shout-Out

I have nothing but love
for my young, talented
throw-back wearing,
record deal anticipating
Number One Draft pick wanna-be
Brothas...
standing on the corner
Monday through Sunday
holding it down as they claim.
Reppin' their hoods
is a full-time job
without benefits or paid vacation.
Still, they do it diligently
never fully understanding
the importance of an accredited education
or the consequences of not having one.
Respect is usually a bullet away,
leaving Baby-Mammas and Grand-Mammas
questioning their faith.
How could God be so cruel,
taking away a son or father?
There is no honor amongst thieves
willing to ascend in ranks

off the wealth and sacrifice of others.
Many of my Brothas
are too impatient to deal
with the hand life has dealt.
Throwing it back with no Spades,
they decide to become monsters
inciting fear while wearing titles...
criminals or menaces
 within a society that deems them
both helpless and hopeless,
erasing their true identities
after persecuting them
for choices they've made
in response to crimes
committed centuries ago.

Yes...I have nothing but love
for my young, talented
Brothas...
of every race
exploiting the gifts God gave them
in hopes of resisting extinction
with each passing day.

As Seen Through Black Eyes

I serve You not
in the name of family tradition
neither for Your long locs of wool
nor because of your darkened complexion,
similar to mine.

I've seen You painted
on the walls of churches
sitting with the Twelve
who walked with You;
hanging from the cross
crowned with thorns,
suffering so that I could live.
This is why I honor You.

Confused now I will confess,
at this talk of Another-
blond-haired, blue-eyed
universally known Imposter.

Election Day: 11/04/08

Hope never tasted so sweet.
Salty tears of joy flood
faces of many colors.
Triumphant smiles and waves
of stars and banners
unify individuals
moved and speechless
overcome with emotion,
demolishing boundaries
to praise his and their victory.
Hope never tasted so sweet
as the night change
came to America.

Barack and Michelle: At Last

When I see them
my heart weakens,
my soul trembles
emotions I can't describe
travel from the top of my head
circling my heart twice
before surging through each limb.

When I see them,
I see love
embraced by many
un-relinquishing in its pursuit
to touch the paralyzed
and move the unmovable
standing fast amidst
a concrete sea of doubt.

When I see them
I am proud to be called
Black, African-American,
Negro, Colored-
everything once shamed, discouraged
unwanted, and underestimated.

When I see them
I see the sacrifices of my parents,
the betrayed faith of my ancestors,
the truth behind lies of equality,
the rewards of choosing wisely,
the power of God
and the importance of prayer.

When I see them
my eyes fill with tears,
and I cry a river
of confidence and satisfaction
knowing that lives have been changed
believers born,
disgruntled appeased,
the mute heard,
the overlooked acknowledged
the discarded empowered
justice served
and a nation of hope
delivered
at last.

Necklace

Words twined tightly
around my neckline
only less decorative
than shiny gifts
meant to be worn.
Accessories enhance beauty,
but this necklace suffocates my soul,
and is a reminder
that words cloaked in hatred
can hang my dreams.

Proud to be American

Nigger? Negro?
Black? African-American?
Perhaps I'm just colored.
My blood runs deep
with no evidence of white stripes
unlike the signs of patriotism
plastered across this nation,
flying on poles, stuck on vehicles,
sewn on clothes.
Proclaiming to the world…
Americans are proud
despite cowardice attempts to destroy
the most powerful democracy
proudly built on the foundation
of *"We the People,"*
omitting the shameful acts that built this land.
Liberty and equality remain in high demand.
Americans are proud
when mourning together
for strangers and the innocent
who continue to become victims
years after those vicious attacks.
Americans are proud

supporting military efforts
seeking revenge, momentarily tabling
differences and dislikes
that have kept this nation
internally enthralled in battle.
Americans remain proud
until this revitalized patriotism
becomes tainted, tattered, and torn
collapsing one-by-one, like the Towers
that fell that tragic September morning.

Stand Your Ground

Pulse racing,
veins enlarged
hate radiating
from their pupils.
Millimeters ending lives
accepted as justified homicide.
White… murderers… walk.
Black… communities… cry.
Justice lifted her skirt
and pleasured herself
while beautiful Black boys,
like Emmitt, Trayvon, and Tamir died.
Heirs to thrones legally lynched
and judicial rights tossed away
as televised trials ripped open flesh
exposing Jim Crow scars.
Crucified people of color become
victims of America's genocide
bought and used like thoroughbreds.
Feigned humility to overcome oppression
sabotaged the image and role of Black men.
Submissive behavior weakened warriors
resurrecting necessity for hymnals and warnings.

The Dark Side of the Butterfly- The Rebirth

Modern day Harriet Tubmans
teaching Black children survival lessons,
arming them with degrees and masks as weapons,
so they can effortlessly blend
in a world that envies and rejects them.
Wading through ignorance and underestimation,
exuding confidence and erudition
never discrediting atrocities of the past.
Determined to right wrongs
with every breath
as if
it
were
their
last.

Soaring High

Sometimes you have to change your latitude
to see the beauty surrounding you…
people surrounding you…
dangers surrounding you…
the obstacles placed in front of you…
gaining leverage on all that tries
to come in between you
and your dreams.

There's peace in knowing
nothing can stop you.
Life ain't always as it seems.
People see the smiles, shares and likes
while you're living your best life.
Only a few know
what it feels like
to be on top.

Sacrifices made to beat your best.
Relationships that can't withstand
the stress of your absence
nor the weight of your success.
Sleepless nights
high on caffeine.
Restless mornings

strategizing your next dream.
Multiple streams of income is a pipedream…
until it happens.

Friends and foe look the same
riding shotgun in lanes you created.
Throwing shade because they failed,
but God… you made it.
Opening doors so we all could eat.
Instead of congratulating,
they'd rather compete
for a spot at a table
with an abundance of seats.

Unafraid to dine alone,
you soar higher than the rest
scouting opportunities
striking at prey.
Your faith keeps you fearless
never looking back.
There's peace in knowing
nothing can stop you.
Walking tall and crying alone
A lifetime of promises and prayer
helped build your thrown.

Sometimes you have to change your latitude
rising to fulfill your destiny
soaring high like an eagle
confident and protected
peaceful knowing

there's NOTHING
that can stop you.

Poet's Warning

Blood drenched pens inspire others
forfeiting personal sanity
while speaking truth
within a forked-tongue society
full of misconceptions
based on mama-always-saids.
Overwhelmed lives create trapped voices
desperate to break,
freeing oneself,
redefining beauty in the eyes of ugliness
black as the pen's ink.
Desperation becomes the muse
destroying one's soul
in hopes of a published ballad.
Beware – gas ovens
do tempt an aching heart!

About the Author

CJ Carter was raised on John's Island, SC. She developed her love for writing poetry at a young age to express her sometimes complicated feelings, thoughts, and emotions. This love for poetry was further developed in high school and later at Queens (College) University where she earned a B.A. in English and Drama with a concentration in Creative Writing. Dark Side of the Butterfly is CJ's debut book of poetry spanning over thirty years of her life, inspired largely by the people she values and her experiences from youth to adulthood.

And now a sneak peek into CJ Carter's next project…

(Book 2)

If These Pages

If these pages could talk
they'd tell all my secrets
revealing fears, shame, and regrets.
They'd affirm the little girl
who found comfort in solitude
building creative and imaginative spaces
after encountering the weight
of being raised to be strong
leaving her feeling overburdened,
overlooked and misunderstood.

If these pages could paint,
they'd display my emotions
in shades of gray
and vibrant hues of purple.
Masterpieces in acrylics and mixed media
gently warming before violently scorching
the canvas of my heart.
Abstract portraits showcasing
the spectrum of my psyche
from vulnerability to rage.

If these pages could sing,
they'd harmonize a chorus
of my accomplishments and successes

creating beautiful melodies
of resilience overcoming failures
a crescendo of triumph
highlighting the times I escaped
suicide's attempts to seduce me
becoming the nothingness
I frequently felt.

But these pages cannot
talk, paint, or sing
so instead they heal me
through my brokenness
releasing anxiety and depression
with alliteration and repetition
reclaiming my strength and power
with autonomy and conviction.
Boldly embracing a whimsicalness
that may not be your cup of tea
but is unequivocally
undeniably
absolutely
me.

www.ingramcontent.com/pod-product-compliance
Lightning Source LLC
LaVergne TN
LVHW071151020225
802669LV00019B/119